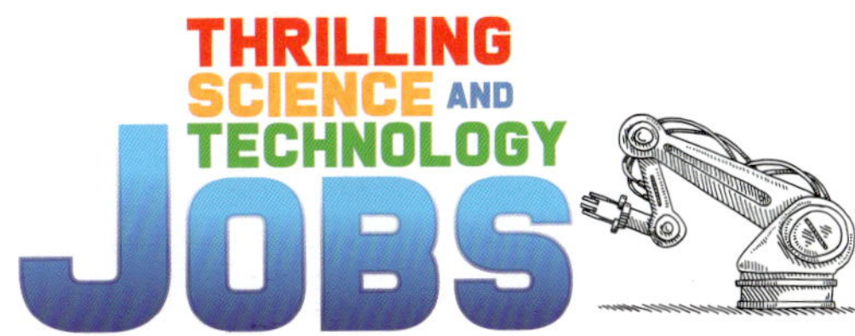

SPACE ROBOT ENGINEERS

Ruth Owen and John Willis

Step 1
Go to **www.av2books.com**

Step 2
Enter this unique code
YCFUMSHJ5

Step 3
Explore your interactive eBook!

AV2 is optimized for use on any device

Your interactive eBook comes with...

Contents
Browse a live contents page to easily navigate through resources

Audio
Listen to sections of the book read aloud

Videos
Watch informative video clips

Weblinks
Gain additional information for research

Try This!
Complete activities and hands-on experiments

Key Words
Study vocabulary, and complete a matching word activity

Quizzes
Test your knowledge

Slideshows
View images and captions

... and much, much more!

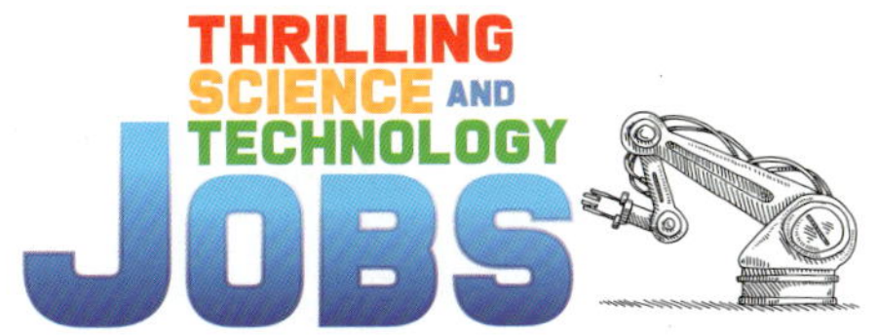

SPACE ROBOT ENGINEERS

Contents

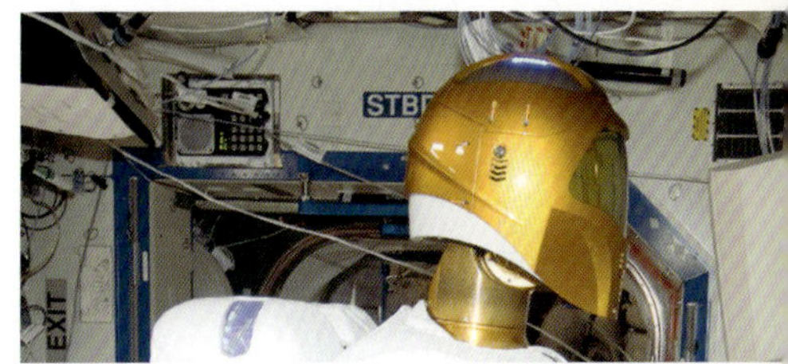

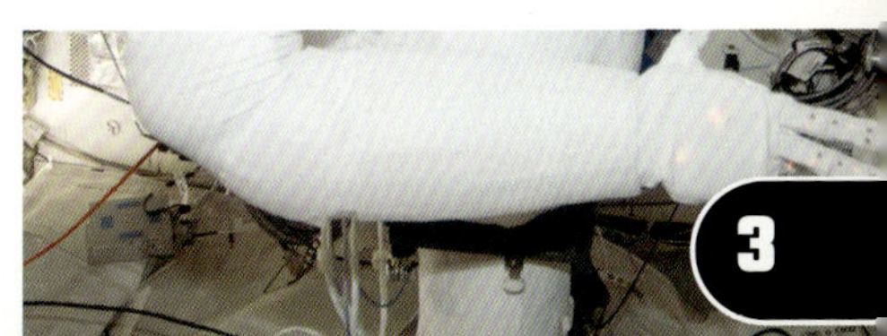

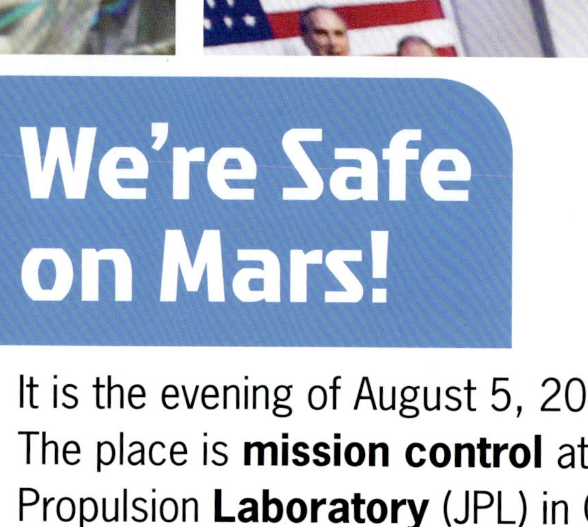

We're Safe on Mars!

It is the evening of August 5, 2012. The place is **mission control** at the Jet Propulsion **Laboratory** (JPL) in California. **National Aeronautics and Space Administration** (**NASA**) scientists, **engineers**, and controllers are watching computer screens and waiting. Millions of miles from Earth, the robot **rover** Curiosity is hurtling toward the surface of Mars.

The final minutes of the robot's journey to Mars slowly tick by. Then NASA engineer Al Chen makes the announcement everyone has been waiting for.

"Touchdown confirmed—we're safe on Mars!"

Mission control erupts in celebration. People cheer, clap, hug, and cry. Tonight is the end of a very long journey. But it is just the beginning of a robot's incredible mission on a distant world.

Thousands of engineers and scientists celebrated Curiosity's safe arrival on Mars.

The Curiosity rover has **17 cameras** on board.

It took more than **10 years** to safely land Curiosity on Mars.

The Curiosity rover has taken more than **620,000** photos of Mars.

Building Space Robots

Mars is a hostile world. It is colder than the Arctic in winter, and its thin air is made up of poisonous gases. It is no place for human explorers and scientists. It is possible, however, for a robot like Curiosity to survive and work in this environment.

Today, robots are used to do work in space that is dangerous for humans to do. Designing and building these space robots is the job of an engineer.

Some space robot engineers are mechanical engineers. They design and build a robot's structure, or skeleton. Electrical engineers work on the electronics that power and control the robot.

Computer engineers design and build a robot's computer "brain." They also write the computer **software** that allows the robot to move, carry out tasks, and even think for itself.

Dextre is a robot that makes repairs on the outside of the International Space Station (ISS).

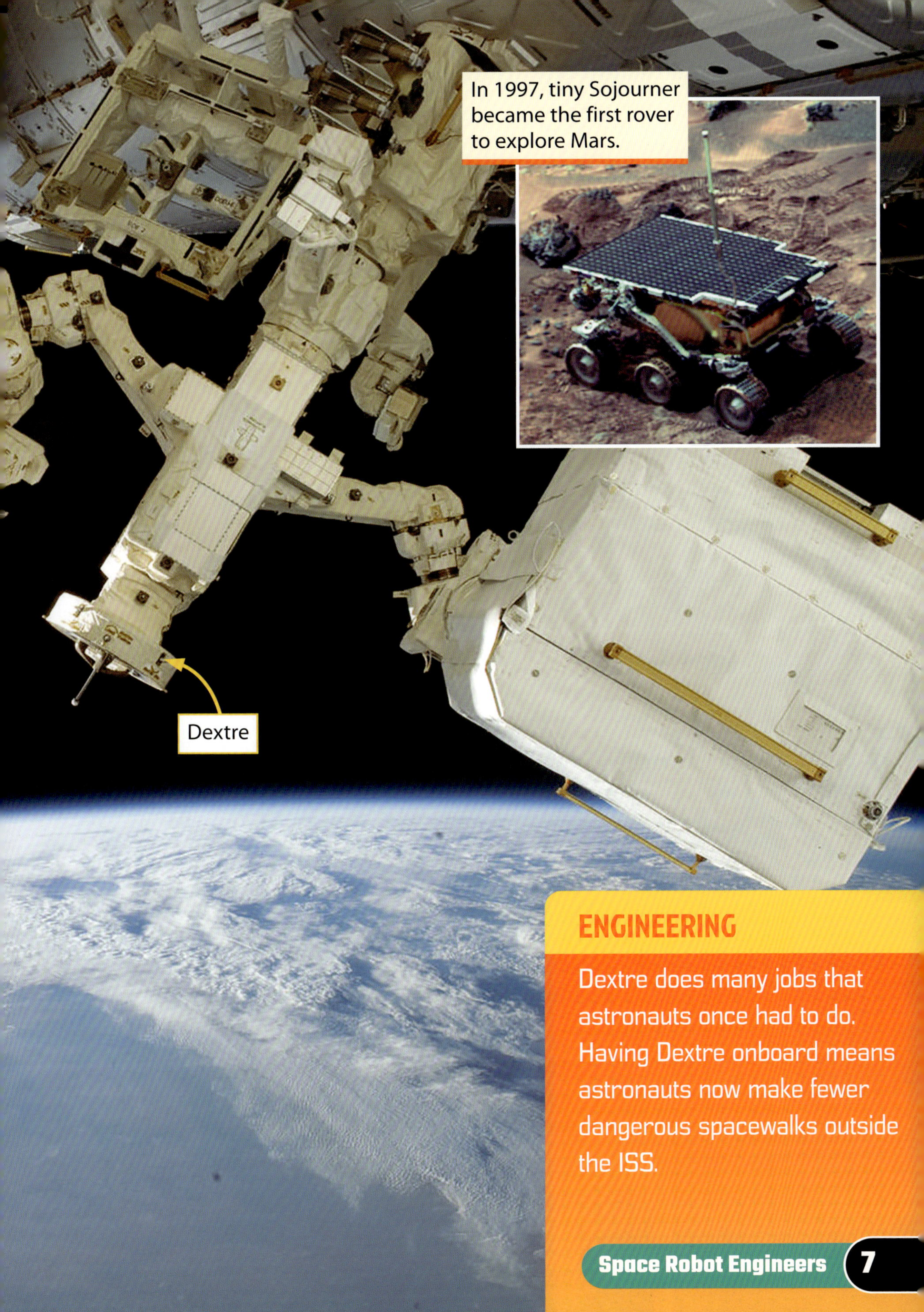

In 1997, tiny Sojourner became the first rover to explore Mars.

ENGINEERING

Dextre does many jobs that astronauts once had to do. Having Dextre onboard means astronauts now make fewer dangerous spacewalks outside the ISS.

How to Design a Robot

How do space robot engineers decide what to build?

Engineers design and build machines that provide a solution to a problem. The problem could be how to fix a space station without endangering its human crew, how to explore a planet that has poisonous air, or how to bring samples back from Mars. The answer to the problem is to build a robot.

Engineers carry out research. What tasks does the robot need to do? How will it get into space? What is the **budget** for the project?

Next, engineers think up design ideas. When several people discuss ideas together, it is often called brainstorming. Once a design idea is chosen, engineers produce plans of the design. The plans might be drawn on paper or created using a computer program.

Then, engineers build a **prototype**, or test version, of the robot. The prototype is tested thoroughly and the test results are analyzed. Often, parts of the design do not work, but this is not a bad thing. When a design fails, it allows an engineer to redesign and improve the robot idea.

Finally, the robot design is fully tested and it is ready to be built for real!

Top Robotics Schools in the United States

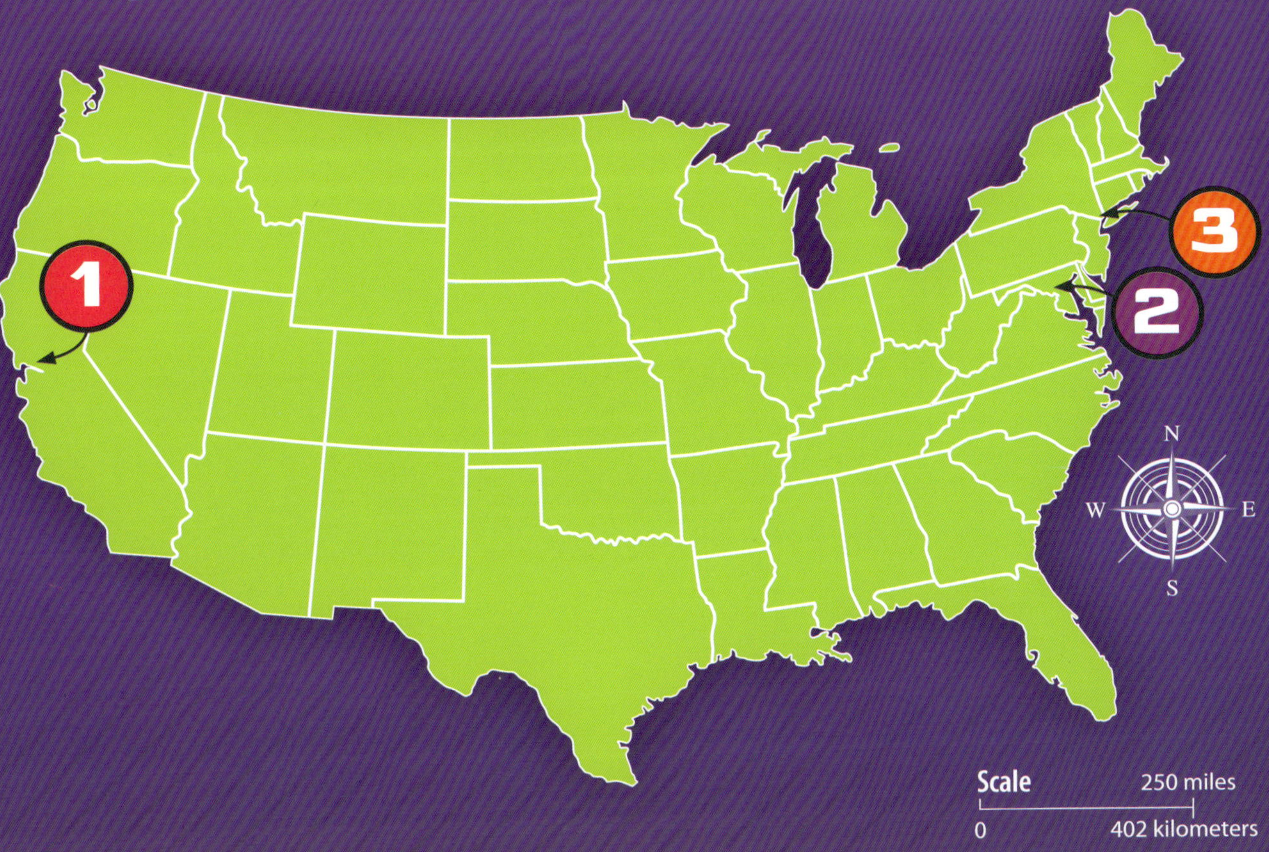

1

2

3

N

W

E

S

Scale 250 miles

0 402 kilometers

UC Berkeley, Berkeley, California
Cassie Cal, a robot at the Berkeley Robotics and Intelligent Machines Lab, has learned how to juggle.

Johns Hopkins University, Baltimore, Maryland
The Johns Hopkins Whiting School of Engineering is a targeted research program. It works with universities and companies around the world in fields including robotics.

Columbia University, New York City, New York
The robotics department at Columbia University focuses on perception, manufacturing, and human-robot interaction.

Designing a Mars Robot

In the late 1990s, a team of engineers and scientists at NASA began work on an exciting new project—the Mars Science Laboratory (MSL) mission. The mission would try to answer the question: Does Mars have, or did it ever have, an environment that could support life? Curiosity was the robot designed by the MSL team to go to Mars and carry out this mission.

Curiosity would be the largest robot to ever land on another world. Just like a mobile laboratory, it would be fitted with a range of scientific instruments. The robot would use the instruments to analyze rocks and soil on Mars. The team's design for Curiosity also included many cameras so the robot could photograph and film the planet's surface—and itself!

Before Curiosity was built, artists created illustrations of it to show the world what it would look like.

Curiosity by the Numbers

Length	:	10 feet (3 meters)
Width	:	9 feet (2.7 m)
Height	:	7 feet (2.1 m)
Weight	:	2,000 pounds (907 kilograms)
Length of arm	:	7 feet (2.1 m)
Top speed	:	100 feet per hour (30 m/h)

ENGINEERING

Water is essential for life. So Curiosity looks for evidence that there was once water on Mars. It also looks for clues that Mars was once home to **microscopic** living things called **microbes**.

Test-Driving Scarecrow

At the same time that it was building Curiosity, the engineering team also built a lighter, stripped-back test version, or "stunt double." It is known as Scarecrow. Scarecrow was built to weigh the same on Earth as Curiosity would weigh on Mars under the planet's lower **gravity**.

On Mars, Curiosity would need to drive up and down slopes. It would have to maneuver over soft sand, hard, compacted sand, and rocky ground. The engineering team had to be sure that Curiosity would not get stuck while traveling on Mars. This would be a catastrophe that could end the mission!

Scarecrow carried out test drives in the Mojave Desert in California. It was also tested at the Mars Yard. This area is a **simulation** of the surface of Mars built at NASA's JPL.

Scarecrow is used to test Curiosity's tires on large objects.

Scarecrow is still hard at work. It tests out maneuvers on Earth. Then, driving instructions are uploaded to Curiosity on Mars.

ENGINEERING

Scarecrow does not have an onboard computer, or "brain." So it was playfully named after the Scarecrow, a character in *The Wizard of Oz* who lacks a brain. During test drives, the robot is connected by a cable to a computer operated by an engineer.

Clean Rooms and Bunny Suits

When Curiosity went to Mars, the mission team had to be sure the robot carried no microbes or bacteria from Earth. International space laws state that humans must not **contaminate** the planets, moons, or other space objects we explore.

Also, microbes from Earth could affect the results of an experiment on Mars. For example, microbes from Earth might get into a sample of Martian soil that Curiosity was testing. Then, the scientists would have to figure out if the microbes were actually Martian or were in fact earthly hitchhikers!

Like all space robots or spacecraft, Curiosity was built in a clean room. This is a laboratory that is kept sterile, or free of bacteria. No contamination from the outside world is allowed to enter.

No one knows how bunny suits got their name. Possibly it comes from one-piece bunny costumes worn at Easter.

Only an engineer's eyes are visible through a bunny suit.

ENGINEERING

An engineer who works in a clean room must wear overalls, a cap, gloves, and a mask. This outfit is nicknamed a "bunny suit." The protective suit stops microbes, skin cells, or hairs from the person's body from contaminating the room.

The EDL Team

As Curiosity slowly came to life, another team of engineers was hard at work building the equipment to land the robot on Mars.

Curiosity is large and heavy, and it would be hurtling toward Mars at 13,000 miles per hour (20,900 km/h). The Entry, Descent, and Landing (EDL) team had a big challenge on their hands. To safely deliver the robot to the surface, they designed a giant parachute and a sky crane. As the EDL team waited in mission control that night in 2012, they watched their plans and ideas come to life.

Curiosity flew to Mars in a craft called an aeroshell. Near the end of its journey, the craft plunged into Mars's **atmosphere**. The aeroshell's heat shield protected the craft from the scorching heat.

Traveling through Mars's atmosphere slowed the craft. Then, the aeroshell's giant parachute was deployed. As the aeroshell got closer to the ground, the heat shield detached and fell away. The descent stage craft and Curiosity dropped from the aeroshell. Rocket boosters powered and controlled the craft's flight. Finally, the sky crane system lowered Curiosity safely to the ground on tethers.

There were a million things that could have gone wrong. Thanks to the skill of the EDL team, nothing did!

Curiosity's aeroshell entered Mars's atmosphere in the last seven minutes of its journey.

Curiosity used the largest aeroshell ever built.

ENGINEERING

The sky crane system allowed Curiosity to land softly without disturbing the thick layer of dust on the ground. The team could not risk having dust cover the robot's cameras or damage its scientific instruments.

The Mission Scientists

Hundreds of scientists from around the world developed and planned Curiosity's scientific mission. They gathered at JPL to witness the robot's landing. Once Curiosity was safely on Mars, the mission scientists worked as a team to carefully test the robot's instruments on Mars for the first time. Then, each day, they planned the robot's work and experiments.

One of the mission scientists was Professor John Bridges from the United Kingdom. John was part of the ChemCam team. This device fires a laser beam that **vaporizes** rock. A special camera captures the flash as the rock is vaporized. Then, light captured by the camera is analyzed to discover what chemicals the rock contains. Certain chemicals can help show if there was once life on Mars.

Curiosity Tools

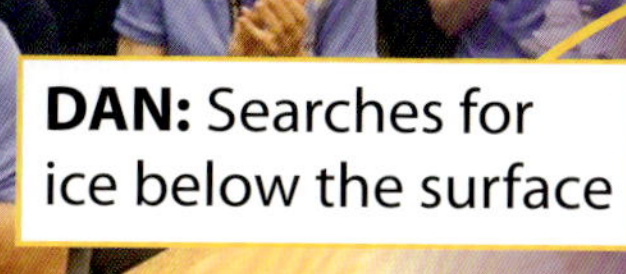

The Curiosity team was finally able to celebrate once it sent back the first photo of Mars.

ENGINEERING

Science is all about asking questions and doing research. As each new photo from Curiosity was downloaded, the mission scientists had lots of new questions and wanted to know more and more!

Driving a Robot Rover

As of early 2020, Curiosity is still hard at work on Mars. The team of engineers that controls the robot is known as the rover drivers.

Earth and Mars are many millions of miles apart. A signal from Earth can take 20 minutes to reach Curiosity. Therefore, it is not possible to give the robot commands and get an instant response. To safely control Curiosity, every second of its day is planned in advance.

Each night, as the Sun sets on Mars, Curiosity takes a break. The team on Earth then works through the night. They plan every inch the robot will travel and every action it will take the next day. Then, Curiosity's "To Do" list for the day is uploaded to the robot.

Curiosity's drivers command the robot to take photos of its tires and other parts. Engineers check these photos for damage to the rover.

Curiosity's drivers use the photos sent back from the rover to plan its course. They check for hazards such as large rocks or holes in the ground.

ENGINEERING

Driving the rover is not done with a joystick or console—just a keyboard. To give Curiosity its instructions, a rover driver keys in hundreds of commands in computer **code**.

Martian Superstars

The engineers that built Curiosity did not get to go to Mars. They did, however, write letters that were put onto microchips and carried into space by their robot.

The teamwork between engineers, scientists, and a robot has made the MSL mission a great success. So far, Curiosity has made several important discoveries.

Curiosity discovered a dried-up streambed. This proved that billions of years ago, streams flowed on Mars. The robot drilled into rock and found tiny amounts of the chemicals carbon, oxygen, hydrogen, nitrogen, sulfur, and phosphorus. These chemicals show that some areas of Mars had environments that were friendly to life.

One day, astronauts may travel to Mars. The amount of radiation on Mars is harmful to humans, though. So Curiosity has studied the levels of radiation on the planet. This research will be used to keep astronauts safe if they go to Mars.

Curiosity takes photos of itself using a camera on its long arm. Images are pieced together from shots taken at different angles, making it possible to leave out the arm.

On **August 5, 2013**, the Curiosity rover sang **"Happy Birthday"** to itself.

Curiosity is the size of a car! It weighs about **2,000 pounds (900 kg)**.

Curiosity takes **samples of rocks** so scientists can **study** them. One sample was **4.2 billion years old**.

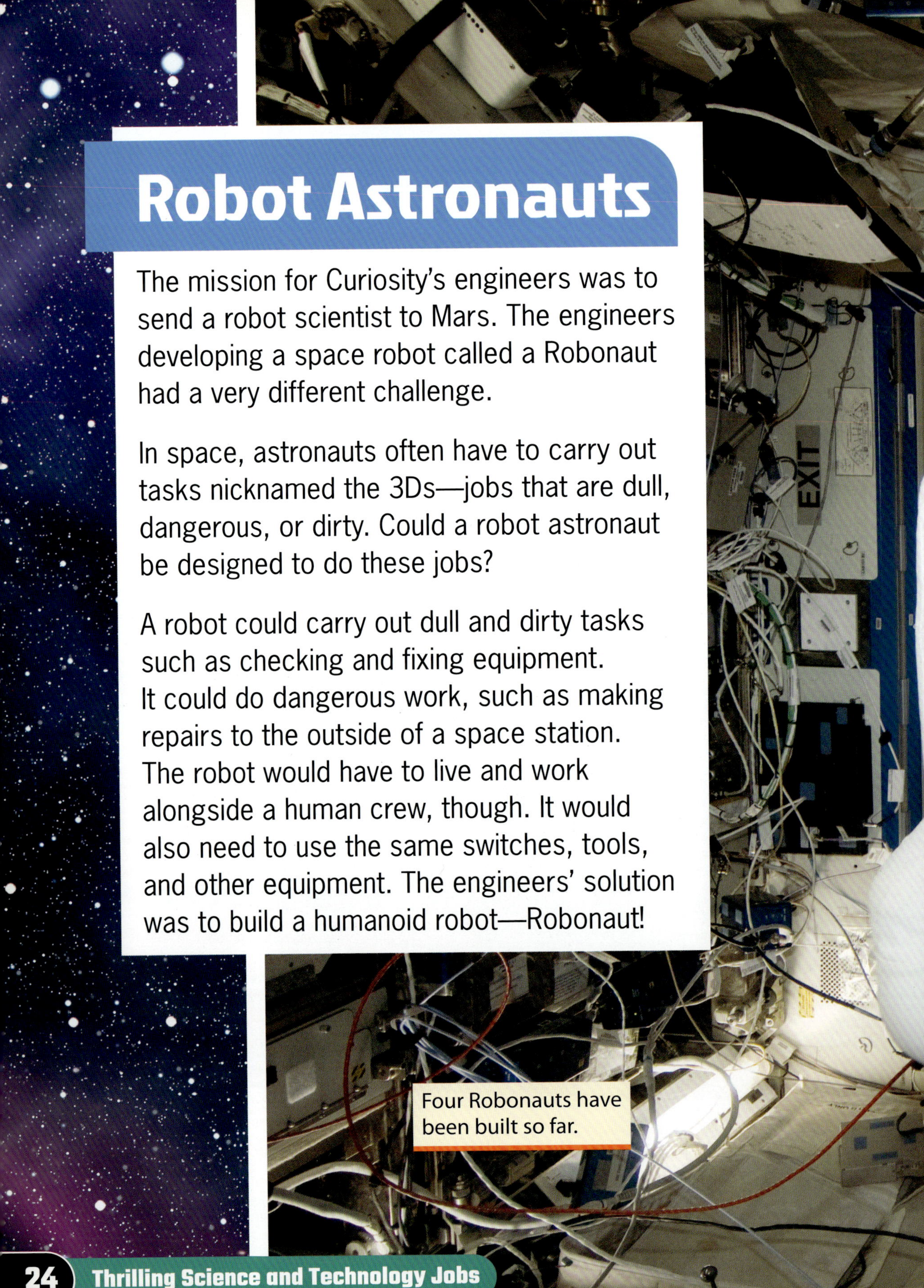

Robot Astronauts

The mission for Curiosity's engineers was to send a robot scientist to Mars. The engineers developing a space robot called a Robonaut had a very different challenge.

In space, astronauts often have to carry out tasks nicknamed the 3Ds—jobs that are dull, dangerous, or dirty. Could a robot astronaut be designed to do these jobs?

A robot could carry out dull and dirty tasks such as checking and fixing equipment. It could do dangerous work, such as making repairs to the outside of a space station. The robot would have to live and work alongside a human crew, though. It would also need to use the same switches, tools, and other equipment. The engineers' solution was to build a humanoid robot—Robonaut!

Four Robonauts have been built so far.

Engineers designed flexible legs for Robonaut 2B with gripping feet called end effectors. The robot holds onto the space station with its feet. This leaves its hands free to do work.

ENGINEERING

In 2011, Robonaut 2B became a crew member on the ISS. Robonaut has now returned to Earth after a seven year mission. In the future, a Robonaut might be sent to the Moon.

Creating Robonaut

To create Robonaut's human-like hands, engineers studied the insides, or anatomy, of human hands and arms. They designed mechanical tendons to control the robot's hands. Tendons are the strong cords that attach human muscles to bones. Robonaut's tendons allow its fingers to stiffen for extra force when it uses a tool such as a screwdriver. If Robonaut is handling a delicate science sample, the tendons can give the robot a softer grip.

Robonaut's head contains cameras that act as the robot's eyes. Its computer brain is actually inside its chest.

Robonaut's engineering team used computers to design the robot. Then, piece by piece, the robot came to life on workbenches in a laboratory.

The Robonaut technology also helped to create a robotic glove and a robotic **exoskeleton**. These creations will help astronauts improve their strength in space.

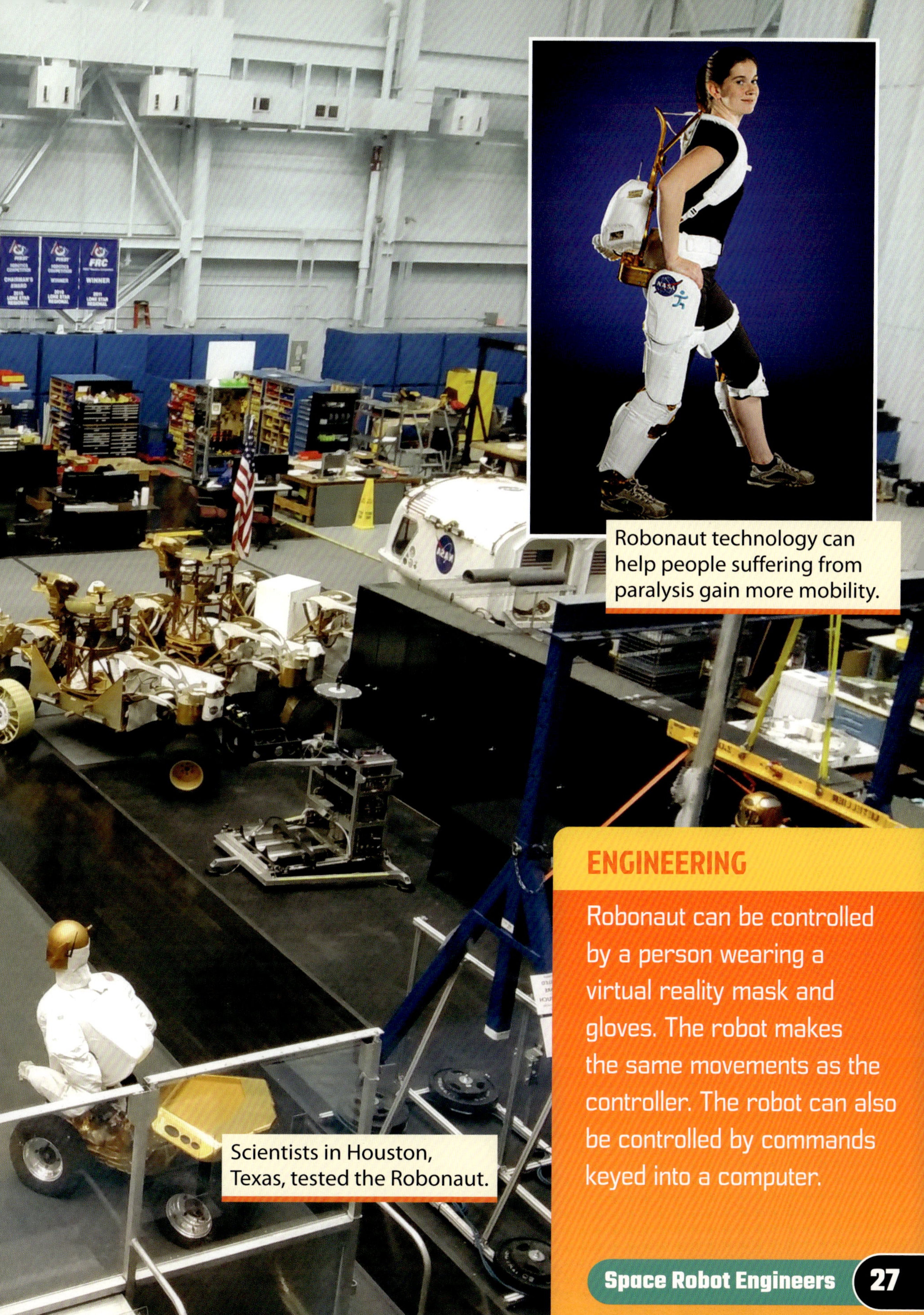

Robonaut technology can help people suffering from paralysis gain more mobility.

Scientists in Houston, Texas, tested the Robonaut.

ENGINEERING

Robonaut can be controlled by a person wearing a virtual reality mask and gloves. The robot makes the same movements as the controller. The robot can also be controlled by commands keyed into a computer.

Space Robots of the Future

What kinds of space robots will the engineers of the future create?

NASA engineers are currently working on plans for Mars 2020. This new robot rover will look similar to Curiosity. Its main science goals are to search for signs of past life, collect rock samples for possible return to Earth, and test technologies for future human missions. Private companies, such as SpaceX, have also begun to create robots for space.

Engineers are working with doctors on a plan to train Robonaut to be a doctor. One day, robot doctors might take care of crews on spacecraft or space stations.

To design and build a space robot, engineers and scientists use technology, science, math, and computer skills. Being an engineer is all about having big ideas—and then bringing them to life!

On November 15, 2018, SpaceX's robot assistant, Crew Interactive MObile companioN (CIMON), debuted on the ISS.

History of Space Robot Engineering

Humans began sending robots to space more than 50 years ago. Since then, many important strides have been made in space robot technology.

1966–1968 Several unpiloted Surveyor spacecraft are sent to the Moon before a manned Moon landing.

1970 Soviet engineers send the Soviet Lunokhod 1 lunar rover to the Moon.

1977 An unmanned spacecraft, Voyager 2, is sent to explore deep space.

1981 The *Canadarm* is installed on the ISS. It helped repair satellites, position astronauts, and move cargo until its final mission in July 2011.

2004 Rosetta, a space probe, is sent to space to intercept a comet, then study it.

August 5, 2012 Curiosity lands on Mars and begins roving.

November 26, 2018 The Insight spacecraft lands successfully on Mars. It will study the deep interior of the planet.

2020 The Mars 2020 project plans to launch.

Space Robot Engineer Quiz

01 When did Curiosity land on Mars?

02 What did SpaceX debut on November 15, 2018?

03 Why was Robonaut created?

04 What was the Scarecrow named after?

05 How much does the Curiosity weigh?

06 How many cameras are on board the Curiosity?

07 What was the first rover to explore Mars?

08 What is the robot that makes repairs on the outside of the ISS?

09 How do scientists safely control Curiosity?

10 What do engineers wear so they do not contaminate spacecraft?

ANSWER

01 August 5, 2012 **02** CIMON **03** To do dull, dangerous, dirty jobs for astronauts **04** The Scarecrow in *The Wizard of Oz* **05** 2,000 pounds (900 kg) **06** 17 **07** Sojourner **08** Dextre **09** They plan out every second of its day **10** Bunny suits

Key Words

atmosphere: a layer of gases around a planet, moon, or star

budget: the amount of money to be spent on a particular project

code: a language of letters, numbers, and symbols used to give instructions to a computer

contaminate: to harm or make something unclean by introducing something dirty or dangerous

engineers: people who use math, science, and technology to design and build machines

exoskeleton: a stiff covering on the outside of the body

gravity: the force that causes objects to be pulled toward other objects

laboratory: a room or building where there is equipment that can be used to carry out experiments and other scientific studies

microbes: living things that are so tiny they can only be seen with a microscope

microscopic: only visible when viewed through a microscope

mission control: a command center on Earth from which people control a space mission

National Aeronautics and Space Administration (NASA): a group of scientists and space experts in the United States; NASA studies space and builds spacecraft

prototype: the first version, or test version, of something, such as a vehicle or machine

radiation: a type of invisible energy that travels through space; high levels of radiation can be harmful to living things

rover: a robot with wheels that is used to explore a moon, planet, or other space object

simulation: a pretend version of something, such as a place

software: the programs that are used to operate computers

vaporizes: turns something into vapor or gas

Index

Get the best of both worlds.

AV2 bridges the gap between print and digital.

The expandable resources toolbar enables quick access to content including **videos**, **audio**, **activities**, **weblinks**, **slideshows**, **quizzes**, and **key words**.

Animated videos make static images come alive.

Resource icons on each page help readers to further **explore key concepts**.

Published by AV2
350 5th Avenue, 59th Floor
New York, NY 10118
Website: www.av2books.com

Library of Congress Control Number: 2019957558

ISBN 978-1-7911-2195-2 (hardcover)
ISBN 978-1-7911-2196-9 (softcover)
ISBN 978-1-7911-2197-6 (multi-user eBook)
ISBN 978-1-7911-2198-3 (single-user eBook)

Printed in Guangzhou, China
1 2 3 4 5 6 7 8 9 0 24 23 22 21 20

032020
101319

Project Coordinator: John Willis
Designer: Terry Paulhus

Every reasonable effort has been made to trace ownership and to obtain permission to reprint copyright material. The publishers would be pleased to have any errors or omissions brought to their attention so that they may be corrected in subsequent printings.

AV2 acknowledges Alamy, Getty Images, iStock, NASA, Shutterstock, and Wikimedia as its primary image suppliers for this title.

First published in 2016 by Ruby Tuesday Books Ltd.